World in Focus
Canada

HODDER
Wayland

HEATHER BLADES

First published in 2005 by Hodder Wayland,
an imprint of Hodder Children's Books
© Hodder Wayland 2005

Commissioning editor: Victoria Brooker
Editor: Kelly Davis
Inside design: Chris Halls, www.mindseyedesign.co.uk
Cover design: Hodder Wayland

Series concept and project management by EASI-Educational Resourcing
(info@easi-er.co.uk)
Statistical research: Anna Bowden
Maps and graphs: Martin Darlison, Encompass Graphics

British Library Cataloguing in Publication Data

Blades, Heather
   Canada. - (World in focus)
   1. Canada - juvenile literature
   I. Title
   971'.07

ISBN: 0750246812

Printed and bound in China

Hodder Children's Books
A division of Hodder Headline Limited
338 Euston Road, London NW1 3BH

Cover top: The skyline of downtown Toronto.
Cover bottom: Tourists approach the Canadian side of Niagara Falls.
Title page: A rally in Montreal against the separation of Quebec from the rest of Canada.

Picture acknowledgements. The author and publisher would like to thank the following for
allowing their pictures to be reproduced in this publication:
Corbis 1 and 24 (Earl and Nazima Kowall), 4 (Staffan Widstrand), 9 (Bettmann), 10, 12 (Sean Sexton
Collection), 13, 37, 46, 48, 58 and 59 (Reuters), *cover bottom* and 15 (Gordon R. Gainer), 16 (Craig Aurness),
17 (Dan Guravich), 20 (Dewitt Jones), 22 and 23 (Jim Young/Reuters), 25 (Carl and Ann Purcell), 26
(Jonathan Blair), 31, 33 and 41 (Paul A. Souders), 32 (l) (Natalie Forbes), 34 (Jeff Christensen/Reuters), 35
(Joseph Sohm, ChromoSohm Inc.), 36 (Baci), 38 and 57 (t) (Galen Rowell), 39 (Vince Streano), 44 (Wolfgang
Kaehler), 45 (Christopher J. Morris), 50 (Gunter Marx Photography), 51 (Laszlo Balogh/Reuters), 56 (W.
Perry Conway), 57 (b) Geray Sweeney); EASI-Images/Roy Maconachie 19 and 40; Mary Evans Picture
Library 8 and 11; Chris Fairclough 5, 14, *cover top* and 21, 27, 28, 29, 32 (r), 42, 43, 47 (l), 47 (r), 52, 53 and 54.

The website addresses (URLs) included in this book were valid at the time of going to press.
However, because of the nature of the Internet, it is possible that some addresses may have
changed, or sites may have changed or closed down since publication. While the author and
Publishers regret any inconvenience this may cause the readers, no responsibility for any such
changes can be accepted by either the author or the Publisher.

The directional arrow portrayed on the map on page 7 provides only an approximation of north.
The data used to produce the graphics and data panels in this title were the latest available at the
time of production.

CONTENTS

1 Canada – An Overview   4

2 History   8

3 Landscape and Climate   14

4 Population and Settlements   18

5 Government and Politics   22

6 Energy and Resources   26

7 Economy and Income   30

8 Global Connections   34

9 Transport and Communications   38

10 Education and Health   42

11 Culture and Religion   46

12 Leisure and Tourism   50

13 Environment and Conservation   54

14 Future Challenges   58

Timeline   60

Glossary   61

Further Information   62

Index   63

About the Author   64

CHAPTER 1

Canada – An Overview

Covering 9,984,670 square kilometres (3,855,081 square miles), Canada is the second-largest country in the world after Russia. From north to south, it extends 4,600 km (2,858 miles), from Alert on Ellesmere Island in the north to the US border near Detroit, Michigan, in the south. East to west, it stretches 5,500 km (3,418 miles), from St John's, on the coast of Newfoundland, to the western border with the US state of Alaska. Canada is surrounded by three oceans, and each of these oceans influences the country's climate, economy and trade links. The Arctic to the north, despite being frozen for much of the year, yields valuable fur and fish resources; the Pacific to the west is important for trade links with the growing economies of South-East Asia; and the Atlantic to the east gives access to Europe and the UK. Canada's only land border is with its main trading partner, the USA, and this boundary is the longest undefended land border in the world.

▼ A villager fishes for Arctic char through a hole in the ice, on Baffin Island, Nunavut.

▲ Pedestrians cross a street in downtown Toronto, Ontario. Like many of Canada's largest cities, Toronto's population is very multicultural.

THRIVING CITIES

The country is made up of seven provinces and three territories, stretching across six different time zones. Its considerable physical size and extreme environments have made settlement difficult and the country's relatively low population is distributed unevenly. The Northwest Territories and Nunavut, the main wilderness regions, together make up a third of Canada's total area (about the same size as India), yet contain only 60,000 people. Most Canadians live in the large cities of Montreal, Toronto, Vancouver and the capital city Ottawa, which are thriving centres of business and leisure. Over 90 per cent of Canada's people live in towns and cities close to the border with the USA. These cities are relatively crowded, with an increasing number of Canadians and immigrants moving to them in search of well-paid employment and a high standard of living.

DIVERSE PEOPLES

Canada has a history of struggles between different groups of settlers, mainly the British and the French, and its indigenous peoples. The country first became a united confederation in 1867, and Canadians mark the event every year on 1 July, Canadian Independence Day. Canada remains predominantly English-speaking but there is a large percentage of French-speaking Canadians and a mixture of different cultures throughout the country. The indigenous Canadian Indians, more commonly known as the First Nations people, make up only 4 per cent of the present population. Around 29 per cent of Canadians are of French origin and the majority of them live in French-speaking Quebec Province. Most Canadians enjoy one of the highest standards of living in the world, with excellent healthcare and education facilities, income and social welfare. However, there are some, such as the First Nations people living on reservations, who do not share these advantages. Many of these indigenous people suffer high unemployment and poor health and housing. The suicide rate in First Nations Inuit groups is three times the national average.

As a resource-rich country, Canada is closely tied to the USA, both as a trading partner and as a political ally. Yet Canada has its own dollar currency, which remains distinct from the US dollar. Although there are many similarities between the two countries, Canada retains closer political ties with Britain (or France in the case of Quebec) than with the USA.

WILDERNESS AREAS

Canada is a country of amazing natural beauty, with vast wilderness areas making up 60 per cent of its land area. Around 10 per cent of the world's fresh water is stored in a vast mosaic of lakes, rivers and ice sheets spread across Canada. Travelling north, where temperatures rarely climb above 0°C (32°F) for much of the year, the subsoil is permanently frozen. Canada's wilderness areas have remained a wildlife haven for many years. They have been only occasionally penetrated by trappers and hunters searching for valuable fur pelts. The Golden Eagle, with a wingspan of over 2.5 m (8 feet), the grizzly bear, wolves and reindeer (or caribou) are just a few of the magnificent creatures found in these remote regions.

Physical geography data

- Land area: 9,093,507 sq km/3,511,003 sq miles
- Water area: 891,163 sq km/344,078 sq miles
- Total area: 9,984,670 sq km/3,855,081 sq miles
- World rank (by area): 2
- Land boundaries: 8,893 km/5,523 miles
- Border countries: USA
- Coastline: 202,080 km/125,492 miles
- Highest point: Mt Logan (5,959 m/19,551 ft)
- Lowest point: Atlantic Ocean (0 m/0 ft)

Source: CIA World Factbook

 Did you know?

Quebec is Canada's largest province, with an area of 1,540,680 sq km (594,856 sq miles). It has a population of almost 8 million, and over 5 million of Canada's 6.5 million French Canadians live there.

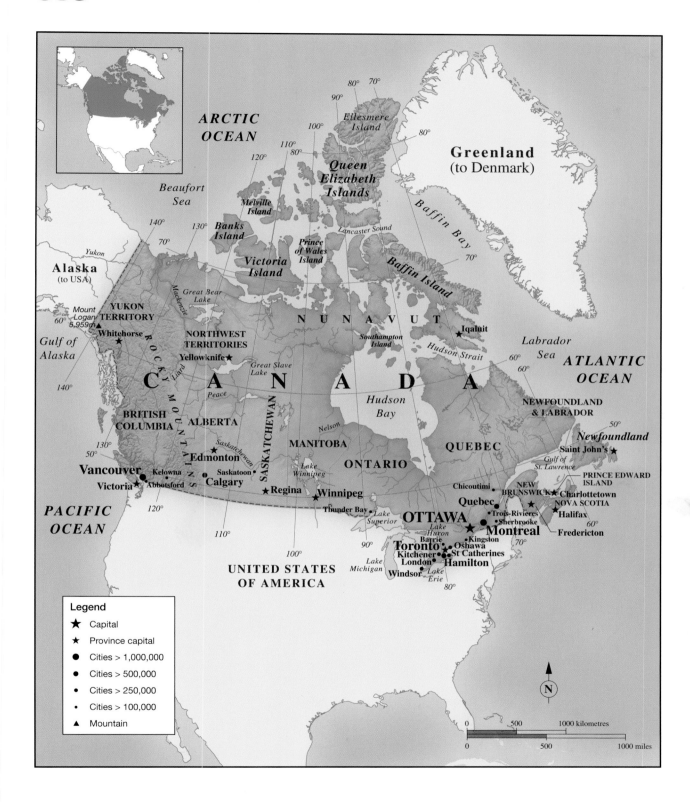

CHAPTER 2

History

The Inuit and North American Indians settled the part of the North American continent that is now Canada around 25,000-30,000 years ago. Originally from Siberia and Mongolia, these first colonizers are thought to have crossed a land bridge connecting Asia and North America at that time. Some of them then moved eastward onto the Plains and south across the remainder of the North American continent.

Ancestors of today's Inuit tribes lived very frugally, hunting and fishing in the frozen north. Meanwhile, the Pacific Coast Indians, with access to abundant supplies of fish, woodland animals, furs and timber, developed distinctive art forms, including totem poles and paintings. The Cree, Assiniboine and Blackfoot tribes of the Plains were nomadic peoples and hunted buffalo, using the meat for food and the hides to make clothing and tepees. Further east, the Algonquin and the Iroquois settled in woodland areas near the St Lawrence River and grew crops like maize, beans and squash.

EUROPEAN EXPLORERS

Vikings landed on Canadian shores over a thousand years ago. These early explorers set up temporary settlements, using them as bases to collect timber and other resources to export to Greenland and Scandinavia. However, by about 1410, after enduring the extreme cold, disease and battles with local tribes, the Vikings had abandoned all hope of permanent

▼ A painting of John Cabot's ship, the *Matthew*, leaving Bristol in 1497. Cabot's journey to Canada was one of many voyages that took place during the age of exploration, as European powers sought riches in distant lands.

▶ Canada's wilderness provided a rich supply of high-quality pelts and many early settlers were fur trappers. They lived in simple log cabins, such as the one depicted in this scene.

settlement in this hostile land. Later, after the success of Columbus's voyage to North America, other Europeans sailed the Atlantic in search of a new route to the spices and treasures of the Orient. In 1497, John Cabot, an Italian navigator, was given permission by Henry VII of England to sail west in search of bounty. Cabot landed on Cape Breton Island, off Newfoundland, but found no spices or treasure – only fish and trees. Nevertheless, fishermen from England, France, Spain and Portugal sailed there to harvest the plentiful cod.

Later, in the 1600s, an even more powerful attraction for European settlers was discovered – furs. British and French fur-trappers flocked to this new land, but clashed with the indigenous people. However, the Europeans soon realized that they needed to trade with and gain knowledge from their new enemies.

Focus on: The French and the British

A French explorer, Simon de Champlain, formed an alliance with the Huron tribe who were traditional enemies of the Iroquois. This heightened the tension between the tribes. On one occasion, some 300 Mohawk (allies of the Iroquois) were massacred by de Champlain's forces and the Huron. After this battle, the Iroquois joined forces with the Dutch and British. During the seventeenth and eighteenth centuries, there were frequent disputes between the French, the British and the indigenous peoples. The French colony was at the heart of a broader struggle between the French and the British for supremacy in North America. In 1713, under the Treaty of Utrecht, Britain gained large areas of eastern Canada, including the valuable Hudson Bay and lands south of the Great Lakes. Later, in 1756, France and Britain began the Seven Years' War (known in North America as the French and Indian War). In 1763, the British army triumphed and France surrendered all its North American territories to Britain.

BIRTH OF A NEW COUNTRY

Until 1867, Canada was a collection of separate British held colonies. The people of these colonies were a mixture of British, French and other recent settlers, along with the original indigenous Canadians. These separate colonies developed their own economies, mainly based on trading and utilizing the local natural resources. Despite these settlements, the areas that remained virtually uninhabited in the middle of the nineteenth century included present-day Yukon, the Prairie Provinces and parts of the Northwest Territories (most of which were still under the control of the British-owned Hudson's Bay Company).

VICTORIA, VANCOUVER'S ISLAND.

▲ This nineteenth-century engraving shows a small steamship anchored near Victoria, on Vancouver Island. In 1843, a Hudson's Bay Company post, Fort Camosun, was founded on the site of Victoria. In 1851, the city was established as the capital of the crown colony of Vancouver Island. It became the capital of British Columbia in 1871.

 Did you know?

While sailing up the St Lawrence River in 1534, Jacques Cartier, a French explorer, is said to have noticed that the First Nations people referred to their settlements as *kanata*, and assumed that this was their name for the entire country.

▲ Fort Garry in Winnipeg, in 1850. Winnipeg first became important as a trading centre for the Hudson's Bay Company and the company still has its headquarters there today. It became a city in 1873.

During the American Civil War (1861-1865), many people in the divided Canadian colonies feared that America might expand northwards and take over valuable land in the Prairies. This threat prompted the three key Canadian politicians of the period – George Cartier, John A. MacDonald and George Brown – to unite Canada as a confederation in 1867. Nova Scotia, New Brunswick and Canada (present-day Ontario and Quebec) were united under the British North American Act. Then, in 1868, the new Canadian government bought Rupert's Land from the Hudson's Bay Company. This agreement brought Manitoba into the confederation, followed by British Columbia (1871), Prince Edward Island (1873), Alberta and Saskatchewan (1905) and finally Newfoundland (1949).

Settling and uniting this vast new land was difficult. Regions that were rich in resources and close to rivers and ports, like those along the St Lawrence River, developed quickly. Meanwhile, inhospitable regions, such as the Yukon territories and parts of the Prairie Provinces, were less attractive to settlers. In attempting to control and develop these more remote regions, the Canadian government often ignored the rights of the First Nations people. For instance, the agreement to purchase Rupert's Land from the Hudson's Bay Company took no account of the indigenous groups occupying the area. These tribes included 5,000 Metis Indians (the mixed-race French-speaking Catholic offspring of aboriginal and early European settlers) who had considered the land theirs for centuries.

▲ Nineteenth-century railway workers with a locomotive belonging to the Canadian Pacific Railway, the first transcontinental transport link.

Some land disputes between the Canadian government and First Nations peoples were settled in the twentieth century. (One of the most significant settlements took place in 1992 and eventually led to the creation of Nunavut Territory in 1999.) But many other land disputes are still being contested.

Did you know?

The Hudson's Bay Company was established in 1670, when King Charles II of England granted the company trapping and mineral rights over the land draining into the Hudson Bay, known as Rupert's Land. The company mainly used the port of York City to export fur pelts to Europe. The North American Fur Auction Company, the direct descendant of the Hudson's Bay Company, still exports furs all over the world.

EARLY SETTLERS

The great Canadian Pacific Railway, built in 1869, helped link the parts of the confederation. Between 1896 and 1913, over a million people used the railway to reach new, unsettled land in the Prairies (bounded by the Rocky Mountains to the west and Ontario to the east), which included Alberta, Saskatchewan and Manitoba.

Canadian government officials went to Europe to recruit settlers. Early migrants to the Prairies were offered 65 hectares (160 acres) of free land and Canadian citizenship, in exchange for a $10 registration fee and an agreement to stay on the land for at least six months of the year for three years in a row. Many of these settlers left Europe to escape economic depression, and looked forward to making a fresh start in Canada. But few were prepared for the loneliness of Prairie life and the extreme Canadian climate, with its hot dry summers and freezing winter blizzards. Nevertheless, settlers flooded into the Prairies, leading to an economic boom in places like Calgary and Vancouver. In 1896, gold was found in Klondike, a river valley in the Yukon Territory. Over the next 15 years, around 30,000 people went there, hoping to make their fortunes, but few settled permanently.

TWENTIETH-CENTURY CHANGES

During the First World War (1914-1918), Canadian soldiers fought alongside British troops against the Germans. The 1917 battle of Vimy Ridge in France was a notable victory for Canadian soldiers, even though it cost over 11,000 Canadian lives. During the First World War, Canadian wheat was in great demand in Europe because cheaper supplies from Russia were unavailable. However, after the war Canada again competed as a wheat producer with Russia, Australia and Argentina. To make things harder, the Prairies, Canada's main wheat-growing area, were hit by droughts during this period, and harvests were poor. In addition, grain prices fell during the 1930s and a deep depression hit the Canadian economy.

In 1931, the Statute of Westminster finally made Canada an autonomous state within the British Empire. This removed the last imperial power Britain had over Canada, meaning that it could no longer make laws for Canada unless it was asked to. Newfoundland did not adopt the statute and remained under British rule until 1949, when it became a province of Canada.

In the Second World War (1939-1945), Canadian soldiers joined the Allied forces (including Britain and the USA). After the war, the Canadian economy began to recover and the country again attracted immigrants. In the twentieth and twenty-first centuries, Canada has taken a leading role in international organizations, such as the North Atlantic Treaty Organization (NATO), a defensive alliance of North Atlantic countries formed in 1949, and the United Nations (UN). Canadian troops also served with British and American soldiers in Afghanistan, in 2001.

▲ A Canadian trooper prepares his gear near a Coyote reconnaissance vehicle at the Edmonton Garrison, in January 2002, while getting ready for assignment to Afghanistan.

CHAPTER 3

Landscape and Climate

Large parts of Canada can be described as wilderness. The interior lowlands around Hudson Bay are said to make up around one-twelfth of the Earth's land surface and 80 per cent of Canada's land area. The central feature of these lowlands is the Canadian Shield, a remnant of some immense granite mountains formed over 500 million years ago. The top layers of the mountains were scraped off by glaciers about 70,000 years ago. The huge 3 m (10 foot) thick glaciers created a saucer-shaped depression, and this depression became Hudson Bay. Some of Canada's best farmland is found in the surrounding lowland area, known as the Prairie Provinces.

LAKES, RIVERS AND MOUNTAINS

The Canadian/US border runs through the five famous Great Lakes of North America, allowing Canada and the USA to share them. Lakes Erie and Ontario are linked to the Atlantic Ocean by the 144 km (90 mile) long St Lawrence Seaway. The St Lawrence, the Mackenzie, the Yukon and the Nelson-Saskatchewan are among the forty longest rivers in the world.

▼ Snow-topped Rocky Mountain peaks, near Kicking Horse Pass, in Golden, British Columbia.

In western Canada, the Canadian Rocky Mountains extend through Yukon Territory and British Columbia, occupying about 13 per cent of Canada's land area. They dwarf the country's other mountains to the east (a northern extension of the Appalachian range). The Rocky Mountains started forming over 200 million years ago, when two vast sections of the Earth's crust collided with each other, and were forced up into a series of huge folds. Since then, glaciers have carved out the classic 'dog tooth' peaks. The Rockies extend approximately 4,800 km (3,000 miles), from Alaska in the north, through Canada and the USA, to Mexico in the south.

▼ Niagara Falls straddles the border between the USA and Canada and is the most visited waterfall in the world. The viewing craft in this picture is approaching the Canadian side of the falls.

FROZEN LANDS

Nunavut and the Northwest Territories, in sub-Arctic northern Canada, are covered with ice during the extended winter, when temperatures can drop to below -51°C (-60°F). Temperatures are so low for most of the year that the sub-surface remains permanently frozen, forming an impermeable layer called permafrost. The thin surface ice melts during the short summer but the permafrost prevents water from draining away, and the landscape turns into a series of vast swamps, rivers and lakes.

 Did you know?

Niagara Falls is actually two waterfalls. The American Falls are 55.5 m (182 feet) high and 328 m (1,076 feet) wide. The Canadian Falls, known as Horseshoe Falls, are 54 m (177 feet) high and 640 m (2,200 feet) wide.

EXTREMES OF CLIMATE

Canada extends through more than 45 degrees of latitude. Its surrounding oceans and high mountain ranges all affect its climate, often causing extreme weather patterns. For example, the far north of Canada experiences Arctic conditions nearly all year round, falling to temperatures of -50°C (-58°F) in winter and receiving an average of 410 mm (16 inches) of snow. In contrast, summer temperatures in Vancouver often reach 30°C (86°F) and onshore winds blowing from the Pacific bring up to 1,529 mm (60 inches) of rainfall in a year.

British Columbia, on Canada's west coast, has the most temperate climate in the country, which encourages the growth of its extensive temperate rainforests. Warm westerly air blows in from the Pacific Ocean and cools as it is forced to ascend the western slopes of the Coastal Ranges and Rocky Mountains, causing heavy rainfall and snow. Further inland, the Prairies have a humid climate that is ideal for growing grain, with rainy springs, hot summers and cold winters.

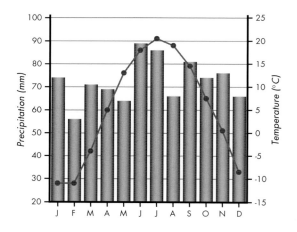

▲ Average monthly climate conditions in Ottawa

▲ Wheat fields in the Canadian Prairies, in Saskatchewan. These flat plains are particularly prone to cyclones or tornadoes, and Canada experiences approximately 80 tornadoes a year. One of the worst was the Pine Lake tornado, in Alberta, which killed 11 people in July 2000.

The St Lawrence region, north of the Prairies and the Great Lakes, is snow-covered for much of the year. Moving towards the North Pole, the summer season gets shorter and winters get longer, with fewer hours of daylight to warm the atmosphere. In the far north, there is no real daylight at all when the overhead sun is positioned at its furthest point south over the southern hemisphere. This 'darkness' may last about six weeks, gradually getting lighter as the spring season approaches.

The area east of the Great Lakes-St Lawrence region, on the Atlantic coast, has Canada's most variable climate. Influenced by air masses passing over the warm Gulf Stream ocean current and the occasional blast of cold air from Arctic regions, St John's in Newfoundland experiences temperatures as low as -5°C (23°F) in winter and average highs of 20°C (68°F) in summer. Meanwhile, Toronto and Montreal, also in this eastern region but sheltered from the cooling effects of the oceans, have summer temperature averages of over 25°C (77°F).

 Did you know?

The permanently white frozen snow cover in the north of Canada reflects much of the sun's light energy back into the atmosphere, which reduces the amount of solar radiation or heat received. This is called the albedo effect.

Focus on: Climate change

Canada's frozen wilderness areas are experiencing a number of problems, which many scientists believe are due to the effects of climate change caused by global warming. For example, on the islands of the Northwest Territories in the Beaufort Sea, ice sheets are thinning and becoming unsafe to travel on, beaches are turning to mud, the permafrost is melting, and there are more thunderstorms (possibly due to the warming of the oceans). The local Inuit communities have learnt, over centuries, to live in extremely cold temperatures but are finding it difficult to cope with these new unpredictable weather patterns. Wildlife is also changing. Species that are common in warmer climates, such as barn owls, geese, ducks and salmon, are now appearing in Canada's frozen north. The number of polar bears, however, is declining as spring comes earlier and autumn later. This change means a shorter period of ice cover and less opportunity for the bears to hunt seals, their main source of food. The polar bears' long-term survival is seriously threatened. Traditional Inuit culture, which is based on hunting polar bears and other animals that depend on the more extreme cold of the Arctic lands, is also at risk.

▼ A young adult polar bear on a field of melting ice in the Northwest Territories.

CHAPTER 4

Population and Settlements

Although Canada is the second-largest country in the world in terms of area, it has a relatively small population – only about 32 million – and one of the world's lowest population densities, with an average of 3.2 people per sq km (or 8.2 people per sq mile). Canada's population is also very unevenly distributed, with more than 65 per cent of Canadians living on the 5 per cent of land that is taken up by the Great Lakes-St Lawrence lowlands.

A MULTI-ETHNIC MOSAIC

Today's Canadians reflect the pattern of settlement over the past 25,000 years. The early Inuit and native Indian (or First Nations) people were the original settlers, followed by Europeans (mainly British and French). More recently, a growing number of Asian people have been starting new lives in Canada. Just over 59 per cent of Canadians speak English as their first language, 23.2 per cent use French and 17.5 per cent use a variety of other languages. The early rivalries between the first French and British settlers are still evident in modern Canada. For instance, Quebec retains a strictly French culture and identity, separate from the rest of the country.

In 1867, the newly formed government encouraged new settlers to occupy the vast open spaces of the empty country. By 1914, Canada had a population of eight million, three million of whom were immigrants from Europe. Today, 15 per cent of Canadians were born in another country and immigration is still encouraged, to

Population data

- Population: 31.7 million
- Population 0-14 yrs: 18%
- Population 15-64 yrs: 69%
- Population 65+ yrs: 13%
- Population growth rate (2000-2005): 0.8%
- Population density: 3.2 per sq km/8.2 per sq mile
- Urban population: 80%
- Major cities:
  Montreal 3,511,000
  Ottawa 1,120,000
  Toronto 5,060,000
  Vancouver 2,125,000

Sources: United Nations and World Bank

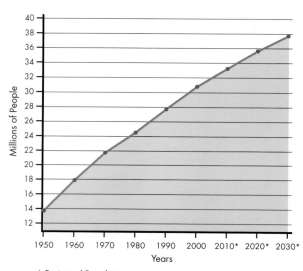

* Projected Population

▲ Population growth 1950-2030

some extent. Most of Canada's recent immigrants come from China, as shown by the growth of large Chinatown districts in Canada's cities. For instance, Chinatown in Vancouver is home to over 100,000 Chinese people and has the second-largest Chinese community outside East Asia. (San Francisco, in the USA, has an even larger Chinese population.)

▲ This store in Vancouver sells Chinese goods. The city has a large Chinese population.

Focus on: Chinese boat people

There has been growing concern in Canada, particularly in British Columbia, about the number of Chinese 'boat people' arriving in the country. Many of these immigrants, who claim refugee status, arrive in poorly maintained ships, which are often only capable of making a one-way journey. They have often used their life savings to pay people-smugglers, known as 'snakeheads', who charge high prices to arrange their illegal journeys. It is estimated that 70 per cent of those claiming to be refugees fail to follow the official procedures for immigrants, and 'disappear' into the close-knit Chinese communities. Canada is a growing economy and needs more workers, but many Canadians feel the immigration controls should be stricter. They welcome a diverse culture but are aware of the need to tighten up on illegal trafficking of people.

FIRST NATIONS PEOPLE

Many First Nations people have become integrated into modern Canadian society. However, some have found it difficult to adjust to the loss of their traditional, rural way of life. In large cities, such as Toronto and Montreal, some First Nations people have found themselves among the most disadvantaged groups in society. Several First Nations communities now live in government-built reservations, and some of them suffer problems linked to crime, alcoholism and drugs.

Many First Nations people have protested to the government about the way it mistreated their people in the past – by taking their land and using them as cheap yet highly skilled labour. (The First Nations people's understanding of their environment was essential to the success of many early enterprises, such as fur trapping.) In 1998, the Canadian government formally apologized for its past mistreatment of the country's native peoples. The government is now making efforts to support First Nations people who are working to preserve their heritage. For instance, Nunavut, with a population of only 25,000, mainly Inuit people, was made a separate territory in 1999, according to the principle of 'aboriginal title', under which ancestral lands are being returned to First Nations people.

? Did you know?

Inuit people rejected the name by which they were commonly known, 'Eskimo', because it means 'eater of meat' and was used by the Algonquin natives as an insult. The word Inuit means 'person'.

The Haida people, who are from the Queen Charlotte Islands, have also regained control of their land. When Europeans first arrived on these islands, in 1774, the Haida population was over 10,000. Today they number about 6,000. Since the Haida Nation won a landmark case in Canada's Supreme Court, the British Columbian government has had to consult with them over land use on their traditional homelands on the Queen Charlotte Islands.

▼ Haida people at a canoe dedication ceremony at Skidegate, on Graham Island, in the Queen Charlotte Islands, British Columbia.

CITY LIFE

Around 73 per cent of Canada's population lives in urban settlements, mostly within 150 km (93 miles) of the US border. Outside this narrow corridor, limited road and rail access has restricted the growth of settlements to a few small isolated towns, and tourist or regional centres such as Whitehorse, Yukon's capital (population 19,058). All Canada's large cities have direct access to the Atlantic or Pacific Oceans, either by canal or by the St Lawrence Seaway, and most have thriving port facilities.

The country's largest city, Toronto (population 4,551,800), is located on the northern shore of Lake Ontario. Toronto is very similar to many large American cities, with streets laid out in a grid pattern (or 'blocks') and a busy downtown business area surrounded by low-rise sprawling suburbs.

Canada's capital is Ottawa (population 863,000), in the state of Ontario. Often considered rather dull, compared with Toronto and Montreal, Ottawa is in fact a vibrant centre that hosts more festivals than any other Canadian city. During the harsh winters, the Rideau Canal running through the city freezes solid and many commuters skate to work!

▲ Toronto's downtown skyline, photographed at night, with Lake Ontario in the foreground.

Quebec City (population 643,200) was the original capital of French Canada. However it is overshadowed by Montreal (population 3,256,300), situated on an island in the St Lawrence Seaway. Montreal is the second-largest city in Canada, the world's largest French-speaking city outside France, and has more historic buildings than any other city in North America. Montreal has an extreme climate, experiencing sub-zero winter temperatures and very hot, humid summers.

Canada's third-largest city, Vancouver (population 1,836,500), is the only significant city on the Pacific coast of the mainland. As the economies of China and South-East Asia expand, Vancouver is becoming increasingly important for Canada's economic growth.

 Did you know?

The UN rates Canada as one of the best countries to live, with its life expectancy and standard of education ranked among the highest in the world.

Government and Politics

Canada is a confederation of seven provinces and three territories. The Oregon Treaty of 1846 fixed the 49th parallel as the boundary between the greater part of the USA and Canada. The Canadian coat of arms includes the Lion, the Unicorn, the British flag and the Fleur de Lys, reflecting Canada's strong historical links with Britain and France.

FEDERAL AND PROVINCIAL GOVERNMENT

Canada is a federal multi-party democracy, with each province voting in its own regional party and an overall majority governing the country. Canada has six political parties and the Liberal Party has been the governing party since 1993. The Prime Minister, Paul Martin, succeeded Jean Chrétien in December 2003 and was re-elected in June 2004 to serve the next five years in office. The country has a bicameral parliament, which means that parliament has two separate 'houses' or sections. There is a Senate of 105 members, appointed by the Governor General; and a House of Commons, with 301 members voted in by the public.

Canada is such a large country, with so many different cultures, that the question of whether different provinces, particularly Quebec and British Columbia, should have their own separate autonomous governments, has been debated many times. Each provincial government is responsible for local taxation, spending and laws concerning social issues, while laws drawn up by the federal government apply countrywide. Each province has powers to pass laws within its own borders but it cannot pass an Act to change its membership of the confederation of Canada.

◄ Canadian Prime Minister Paul Martin (left) stands with US President George Bush during the Summit of the Americas in Monterrey, Mexico, in 2004. Leaders of 34 nations met here to discuss a wide range of regional issues, especially economic policies.

CANADA'S PRIME MINISTERS

Canada's political system, modelled on the British style of government, has a prime minister at its head. The title 'prime minister' comes from the Latin phrase *primus inter pares* (meaning 'first among equals'). The prime minister is therefore a leader, or first among equals, in the government cabinet of ministers and first among the people of the country.

There have been 21 prime ministers in Canada since 1867, beginning with John Alexander MacDonald, who served for six years. The longest-serving prime minister was Pierre Trudeau who stayed in office for two terms, from 1968 to 1979 and from 1980 to1984 (a total of over 15 years in office). Not all Canada's prime ministers have served their full term of office, and Canada's only woman prime minister, Kim Campbell, served for less than six months, between June and November 1993.

Only two of Canada's prime ministers, John Alexander MacDonald (1878-1891) and John Sparrow David Thompson (1892-1894), have died in office. Others have retired from office or have served as opposition leaders when their government has been voted out of office.

Focus on: Self-government by indigenous people

In 1999, the territory of Nunavut was created on land that was formerly part of the Northwest Territories. This new state was founded by the Canadian government partly as a way of compensating for previous mistreatment of Inuit communities. There are some 50,000 Inuit people in the north and this is the first state to be governed by indigenous Canadians in modern history. In addition, since the late 1970s, Inuit people along the Labrador coast have been campaigning to claim control over their ancestral lands – part of a sparsely populated area covering over 72,500 sq km (27,992 sq miles).

◄ Assembly of First Nations Chief Phil Fontaine (left), who is Anishinabe (Ojibwe or Chippewa) from Sagkeeng First Nation in Manitoba, meets Ottawa government ministers in 2004 to discuss problems with the healthcare system.

▲ Part of a crowd of 150,000 Canadians rallying in Montreal, in 1995, against the separation of Quebec from the rest of Canada. Many in the crowd wave Canadian flags.

INDEPENDENCE FOR QUEBEC?

Conflict between French and British Canadians began in 1759, when the British won the battle for supremacy in North America on the Plains of Abraham just outside Quebec City. At this point, Quebec was formally granted to Britain and made part of British North America. Over the next 200 years, conflict between the British and French in Quebec persisted. When Canada became a confederation in 1867, the province of Quebec was established, with both English and French as its official languages.

During the 1960s, there was a growing movement, led by artists, writers and politicians, including then Prime Minister Pierre Trudeau, in favour of Quebec separating from the rest of Canada. A separatist political party, the Parti Quebecois (PQ), was formed in 1968. The PQ gained control of Quebec's provincial government and made French the official language of the province in 1976.

 Did you know?

The slogan of separatist campaigners 'Vive Le Quebec Libre!' (meaning 'Long Live Free Quebec') came from the French President Charles de Gaulle when he visited Quebec in 1967.

Since the PQ came to power, the previous dominance of Anglophone (English-speaking) people in Quebec's government, its civil service and its businesses has been reversed, in favour of Francophones (French-speakers). Many new Francophone businesses were set up through a project called 'Quebec Inc' which supported French-speaking businessmen. Higher education opportunities for Francophones were also expanded. Quebec now has four French-language and three English-language universities. In addition, French Canadians in Quebec earn slightly more on average than English Canadians in the province. At the same time, many English-speaking businesses have left Montreal and Quebec and moved to Toronto. This has caused some unemployment in Quebec and has increased the need to attract more industry to the province.

 Did you know?

Public signs in Quebec have to be in French and English. On many unofficial signs, there is no English at all.

The PQ has continued to strive for Quebec's independence from the other provinces of Canada. However, although the PQ is now the party in power in Quebec, the province is still part of Canada. The people of Quebec have been given two opportunities to vote on this issue. The last one was in 1995 and separation was narrowly rejected.

▲ All signs in the province of Quebec appear in both French and English. Many of the French-speaking people of Quebec would like Quebec to be independent.

CHAPTER 6

Energy and Resources

Canada is one of the most resource-rich countries in the world, and it was the fifth-largest energy producer in 2001 (after the USA, Russia, China and Saudi Arabia). Energy production is Canada's second-largest industry, and it includes uranium (used in the production of nuclear power), fossil fuels such as oil, coal and natural gas, and hydro-electric power (HEP).

▲ Massive machinery scoops up the black tar sands, from which oil will be extracted, in a huge open-cast mine in Athabasca.

Energy data

- Energy consumption as % of world total: 2.8%
- Energy consumption by sector (% of total)

Sector	%
Industry:	40
Transportation:	29
Agriculture:	2
Services:	13
Residential:	16

- CO_2 emissions as % of world total: 2.1
- CO_2 emissions per capita in tonnes p.a.: 16

Source: World Resources Institute

Focus on: Oil sands

In the isolated Fort McMurray area, on the Athabasca River, northern Alberta, there is a reserve of some 11,600 sq km (4,478 sq miles) of sticky, black, bituminous oil sands. Amid growing fears of diminishing oil reserves, rising prices and possible disruption of supplies from the Middle East owing to continuing instability in countries such as Iraq, the oil sands of the Athabasca could perhaps offer a secure, affordable oil supply for North America. However, the crude oil extracted from the sands is much thicker than conventionally drilled oil, and therefore involves higher transport and refining costs. It is also difficult to get people to work in such inhospitable wilderness areas without paying high wages. Furthermore, the refining process produces far higher levels of CO_2, which will make it difficult for Canada to reduce its emissions in line with the targets set at the Earth Summit in Kyoto, Japan, in 1997. The Canadian oil company, Petro-Canada, is searching for ways around these problems, but the environmental and financial costs of securing long-term oil supplies from the sands of Athabasca could turn out to be very high.

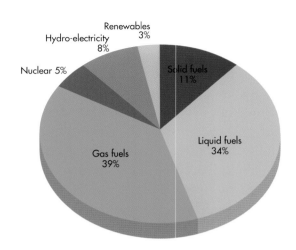

▲ Energy use by type

ENERGY PRODUCTION

Canada has huge natural gas reserves and is the world's third-largest producer, providing about 87 per cent of the USA's natural gas supply. Coal is also an important export, much of it going to Japan and South Korea. Canada's proven oil reserves in 2004 were 178.9 billion tonnes (176 billion tons) – one of the world's largest reserves. Most of the oil is produced in Alberta and the western provinces, but most is consumed in Ontario and the eastern provinces.

Canada is also one of the world's largest producers of hydro-electric power (HEP), and this form of electricity supplies 61 per cent of the country's needs. Quebec and Ontario produce their HEP from large fast-flowing rivers. However, there has been some concern about the damage this causes to Quebec's environment. Many forest areas have been cleared, and land has been flooded, in the process of constructing large dams for HEP schemes. In addition, much of this land was previously occupied by First Nations people, who have been forced to leave.

Around 21 per cent of Canada's electricity is generated by fossil fuel power stations (using coal, oil and gas), and nuclear energy provides 17 per cent. Keen to meet its Kyoto target (a 6 per cent reduction in its CO_2 emissions by 2010), Canada is trying to develop renewable forms of energy, such as wind power which uses turbines to convert the wind's energy into electricity. Another renewable form of energy involves photo-voltaic (PV) cells, which can be mounted in solar panels to convert the energy of the sun into electricity. Even though solar and wind power produce only 1 per cent of Canada's electricity at present, they are particularly well suited to isolated communities, where the cost of connection to the national grid is high.

▼ Revelstoke Dam, on the Columbia River, is one of many large dams that have been built in Canada to generate hydro-electric power (HEP).

ENERGY CONSUMPTION

Many Canadians drive powerful vehicles, which use large amounts of fuel. They need to keep warm in the extremely cold winters and cool in the often humid, hot summers. All these requirements add up to heavy energy consumption. In fact, Canadians are the eighth-highest energy consumers in the world.

As Canada is so rich in energy resources, it exports over 31 per cent of what it produces to the USA – mainly in the form of electricity. The importance of the energy link between the two countries was clearly demonstrated in August 2003, when power cuts in the Great Lakes-Ontario area and the north-east states of the USA caused major disruption. Apparently, an extraordinarily high demand from air-conditioning units in northern Ohio during this hot August period overloaded grid supply lines, resulting in a shut-down of supply in the wider region.

MINERALS AND OTHER RESOURCES

Canada also has abundant deposits of metal ores and minerals. During the 1890s, there was a gold rush in the Yukon and British Columbia, when thousands of people from all over the world came to the region's Klondike area. Today, Canada is known as the world's largest producer of zinc and the second-largest producer of nickel. Other ores, such as copper, potash, asbestos, gypsum and coltan (used in the manufacture of circuit boards), are also mined in the country. In addition, Canada is the world's largest exporter of timber products and wheat, and Canada's oceans, lakes and wildernesses hold vast numbers of fish and animals with fur pelts.

◄ Highland Valley Copper Mine, in the Rocky Mountains, is one of the world's largest copper mines, processing 35,560 tonnes (35,000 tons) of copper a day.

TIMBER PRODUCTION

Around 50 per cent of Canada is covered in forest. The coniferous forests of the north make up approximately 80 per cent of Canada's total forests. The remainder consists of 'old growth' rainforests on the west coast of British Columbia and Vancouver Island, and the deciduous forests of the east.

Focus on: Rainforest of the North

The Pacific Temperate Rainforest on Vancouver Island, off the west coast of British Columbia, produces ten times more wood than the South American rainforests. The huge trees in this forest, including sitka spruce, cedar, spruce and Douglas fir, are very valuable. A single sitka trunk can fetch up to $60,000.

This rainforest once stretched from Alaska to northern California. However, deforestation is a major environmental problem in Canada, especially in British Columbia and Vancouver Island. The forests are being removed by 'clear cutting' (clearing all the trees in an area and leaving the land exposed), which is particularly damaging. Important habitats are destroyed and soils are left exposed to rainfall, causing serious soil erosion. Environmental campaigners continue to try to raise public awareness of these issues.

▼ A female forester at work in a forest north of Nanaimo, on Vancouver Island.

CHAPTER 7

Economy and Income

Canada has a huge wealth of resources and a relatively low population to make use of them. This is partly why Canada is one of the most important trading nations in the world. It is also well located to trade with some of the world's strongest and fastest-growing economies, particularly the United States, China and South-East Asia.

IMPORTS AND EXPORTS

The Canadian dollar has been weaker than the US dollar in recent years, making Canada an attractive trading partner for the USA. This healthy trading position has earned Canada a trade surplus; the total value of Canada's exports is higher than its imports. Most of Canada's exports are raw materials and the bulk of its imports are manufactured goods.

Economic data

- Gross National Income (GNI) in US$: 756,770,340,864
- World rank by GNI: 8
- GNI per capita in US$: 23,930
- World rank by GNI per capita: 24
- Economic growth: 2%

Source: World Bank

In 1989, the USA, Canada and Mexico formed the North Atlantic Free Trade Agreement (NAFTA). This agreement, which came into effect in 1994, allows the three countries to trade with each other without having to pay import or export taxes. This has led to a growth in trade for all three countries and a strong demand for Canadian products. It has also increased the volume of goods that Canada imports from Mexico and the USA. In 2004, Canada was Mexico's second-largest market for exports.

FORESTRY AND AGRICULTURE

Canada's forest products industry provides jobs for over a million Canadians and it brings in 55 billion Canadian dollars annually. Two-thirds of this income comes from lumber, plywood and wood products, and the remaining third from pulp and paper. Around half the world's newspapers are produced using paper made from Canadian trees and the country is the world's largest supplier of paper-grade pulp, exporting 80 per cent of what it manufactures to over 100 countries. The largest customer is the USA, followed by Japan, China and Britain. As demand for printing paper increases, the industry is responding by using

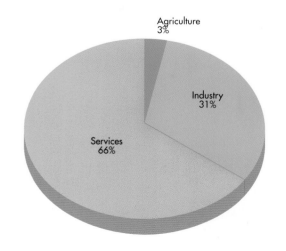

▲ Economy by sector

more recycled paper. Around 75 per cent of Canadian pulp is made of either recovered paper or wood chips and residue, which would previously have ended up in landfill sites. The process of making pulp involves either mechanically or chemically separating out wood fibre, and this uses large amounts of water and energy. The Forestry Products Association of Canada is working to promote more environmentally sensitive ways of managing the industry. For instance, they are decreasing the use of fossil fuels. They are also including more First Nations people in management partnerships as part of their inclusion policy.

Another important sector of the Canadian economy is agriculture, which employs a lot of people on farms and in related industries, such as transport, processing and the manufacture and maintenance of farm equipment. Most of

Canada's cultivated land lies within 500 km (300 miles) of the US border. Canadian farm products include livestock, fruit, tobacco and potatoes, but Canada is probably best known for its grain crops. It is the second-largest exporter of grain in the world. Around 75 per cent of the country's cultivated land is in the Prairies, with Saskatchewan growing two-thirds of the country's wheat. Transport links are very important to this export industry. Trains take the grain westward to Vancouver for export to the Japanese and East Asian market, and eastward to Churchill and Thunder Bay on the Great Lakes-St Lawrence Seaway for export to the European markets.

▼ Grain is emptied from a tractor-driven combine into a trailer during the harvesting of a wheat field at Ebenezar, in Saskatchewan, Canada.

Focus on: The fishing industry

Canada's fishing industry was worth more than $5 billion a year in 2002, and it exports over 75 per cent of its fish each year. The Atlantic catches provide 82 per cent of the total, 14 per cent come from the Pacific fisheries, and 4 per cent from freshwater sources. Atlantic lobsters are Canada's most valuable seafood product, and hake, salmon, clams and halibut are also important. In 1992, a ban was imposed on fishing cod off the Atlantic Grand Banks because of falling fish stocks. This ban encouraged the growth of fish farming (or aquaculture) which accounted for 14 per cent of total Canadian fish production in 2002. However, there are growing concerns about the environmental impact of fish farms. Farmed salmon are often kept in open net cages in the sea, and excess food and organic waste pollute the ocean bed.

▲ A worker harvests salmon by netting them from a pen on a fish farm in British Columbia.

MANUFACTURING AND SERVICE INDUSTRIES

Around 67 per cent of Canada's gross domestic income is generated by service industries and 32 per cent by manufacturing. The main manufacturing industries in Canada are processing timber, pulp and paper; chemicals;

▲ A pulp mill at Alberni, on Vancouver Island. These mills need massive volumes of water to manufacture the pulp.

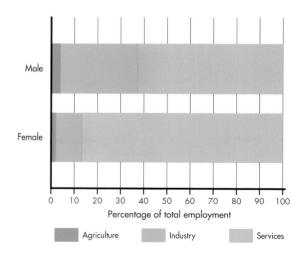

Percentage of total employment

Agriculture   Industry   Services

▲ Labour force by sector and gender

▶ A finishing mill operator sits at the control panel at Algoma Steel Mill, in Ontario. Thick steel blocks are reheated to a nearly molten state, then run at high speed through a series of mills. The molten steel appears as a bright orange band seen through the control room windows.

and metals. The provinces of Ontario and Quebec, in the Great Lakes-St Lawrence region, are Canada's major industrial areas. Cheap hydro-electric power (HEP), a comparatively dense population, easy access to the USA, and transport via the Great Lakes and St Lawrence Seaway are all factors that have helped industry to thrive in this region. Montreal is an important centre for the manufacturing of clothing and Toronto specializes in aircraft manufacturing. The country's automobile and truck industry is also located in this area, fed by the huge steel manufacturing works at Hamilton, commonly known as 'Steel City', on the shores of Lake Ontario.

Did you know?

Canadians save more money per head and buy more insurance than the people of any other nation in the world. This provides plenty of business for their growing finance industry.

Japanese and South-East Asian companies account for about 12 per cent of investment in Canada's businesses. However, when new businesses want to expand in North America, many find Canadian production costs too high and set up in the USA or Mexico instead, where labour and production costs are lower.

One particular area of growth is in finance-related services, such as banking and insurance, centred in the major cities. Tourism is another important industry, with many attractions and a considerable customer base, including both Canadians and visitors from abroad. The tourist industry is well supported by the Canadian government. Canada's film industry is also growing fast, with Vancouver and Toronto both laying claim to the title 'Hollywood North'. Vancouver is an ideal location for American filming companies, because it looks like a typical North American city. It has a mild climate all year round and is far cheaper than using a location in the USA.

CHAPTER 8

Global Connections

As an important economic power in the world, Canada has been one of the G8 industrially developed democracies since 1976. Heads of government and major industrial leaders from these countries meet regularly to discuss a whole range of issues, including international trade regulation with developing countries, environmental questions, terrorism, arms and drug controls.

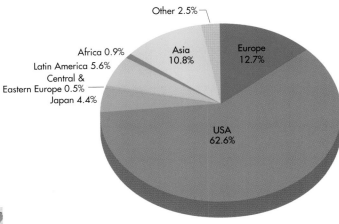

▲ Origin of imports by major trading region

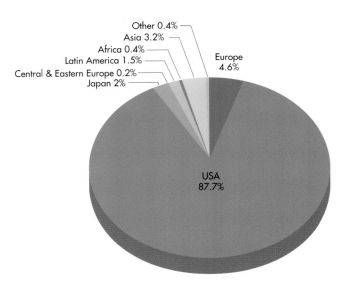

▲ Destination of exports by major trading region

◀ Canadian Prime Minister Paul Martin (left) meets United Nations Secretary-General Kofi Annan at United Nations headquarters in New York, in 2004.

CANADA, BRITAIN AND FRANCE

As a Commonwealth country, Canada retains strong links with Britain. The British queen, Elizabeth II, is the country's Head of State and the Canadian government is modelled on the Westminster government and legislation system. However, Canada no longer has any political allegiance to the UK government. And in 1982, all powers relating to Canada in British law were ended, a further recognition of Canada's independence. The links between Quebec and France are only through language, culture and religion; there are no political ties.

CANADA AND THE USA

The relationship between Canada and the USA is very amicable on the whole. However, there are occasional disputes, as two countries sharing a border are inevitably affected by each other's actions. Resource exploitation and pollution have been particular causes of contention. For instance, Canadians have a long-standing dispute with some industries on the US side of

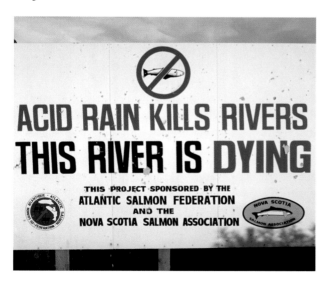

▲ Nova Scotia fishing organizations warn people of the danger of acid rain and the toxic effect on a local river and salmon runs.

the border, which pollute the atmosphere. Pollutants such as sulphur dioxide and nitrogen oxide mix with water vapour in the air to form an acidic solution known as acid rain, which damages Canadian forests. Oil spills and pollution from Alaskan pipelines and ports have also affected Canadian wildlife.

However, Canada co-operates closely with the USA on most defence issues and was a founder member of the North Atlantic Treaty Organization (NATO), through which it pledges support for other NATO members in times of conflict. Canada became a member of the United Nations (UN) in 1945 and Canadian soldiers have served in many conflicts as members of UN peacekeeping forces, including those in Afghanistan and in the former Yugoslavia. Eleven Canadians died in the terrorist attacks on the United States on 11 September 2001. Since then, the USA and Canada have been fighting the 'War on Terror' together, through increased vigilance along the 8,000 km (5,000 mile) border between them. There is also greater security checking on people entering both countries from outside.

Nevertheless, the Canadian government did not support President George W. Bush's decision to invade Iraq in 2003. In recent years, all NATO members have been cutting back on defence spending and have been switching their efforts to rapid reaction, rather than long-term peacekeeping strategies. Canada withdrew all its peacekeeping troops from European bases in 1992 and more recently, in 2004, Canada called many of its troops home from peacekeeping posts in other parts of the world. For example, Canadian troops made up a quarter of the UN peacekeeping force in the Caribbean island of

▲ In this photograph, taken in 1994, a major in the Canadian armed forces walks with Rwandan children in Kigali, who have been displaced because of the Rwandan civil war.

Haiti, which has suffered several coups. Now all those soldiers, along with further troops from Bosnia and Afghanistan, are being recalled. Despite these cutbacks, the Canadian government remains committed to peace initiatives and is a leading campaigner against anti-personnel landmines. A treaty to ban their production, export and use was formally ratified by 141 countries in Ottawa in 1997. Canada has also funded an aid package to train 30,000 Iraqi police in the new independent Iraq.

THE SCANDINAVIA OF THE NORTH?

Scandinavian countries are well known for their generous contributions to aid programmes for developing countries. In the twentieth century, Canada also had a very good record as a donor country and was sometimes called the 'Scandinavia of the North'. However, in more recent years, Canada has not ranked among the top donor countries. For example, in 2003, Norwegians gave US$307.95 per head, compared with US$40.36 per head from Canadians in overseas development aid. Canada's aid donations continue to fall short of the UN aid target, of 0.7 per cent of Gross National Product (GNP), and it is positioned 12th out of 22 in the United Nations generosity league. However, Canada made the fifth-largest pledge of government aid to the Tsunami Disaster Fund in January 2005, with a total of

US$340,644,000 (equal to US$10.71 per person). The Canadian International Development Agency (CIDA) used to be heavily committed to aid programmes in the Horn of Africa. Some of these projects were very successful but other aid programmes have been criticized for appearing to benefit Canadian manufacturers of machinery and materials more than the intended recipients of the aid.

The Wheat Project in Tanzania during the mid-1990s was a case in point. Areas farmed by the indigenous Barabaig cattle farmers were instead used to grow wheat on a large scale in an attempt to improve food supplies. However, this type of farming required expensive equipment. At first, this equipment was donated by Canadian firms. However, later on, any additional or replacement equipment had to be paid for by the Tanzanian government. Canadian agricultural machinery manufacturers benefited from the sales, while the Tanzanian

government's debts increased. Meanwhile, the cattle farmers had lost their land but the wheat grown was too expensive for local people to buy.

The agency now plans to concentrate its work in Africa on health and nutrition, basic education, treatment of HIV/AIDS, and protection of children. Non-government organizations, such as Canadian Oxfam, are also very successful in African countries. Canada is now directing more aid towards Asian and East European countries.

▲ An Afghan worker lifts a bag of wheat donated by a Canadian agency in Peshawar, in 2001.

Did you know?

Voluntary aid programmes show Canadian individuals to be very generous. In a 2004 appeal for people suffering in the Darfur area of Sudan, the Canadian Auto Workers alone raised $150,000.

Focus on: CIVA

Canadian Village India (CIVA) is one of many non-profit-making charitable societies in Canada. Based in Vancouver, CIVA collaborates with agencies and organizations working in rural India, encouraging improvements in education and

healthcare and campaigning on environmental issues, and rights for women and children. For instance, they began working in ten isolated villages in the region of Kutch after an earthquake in 2001, helping children gain access to education.

CHAPTER 9

Transport and Communications

Distance has always been a major obstacle for people in Canada. The extreme climate and hostile landscape have made it almost impossible to build roads and railways in some areas. Much of the country north of the 50th parallel is covered by large lakes and swamps which freeze over during the long winters. Communities in remote areas largely depend on single-engine aeroplanes for contact with the outside world. Canada has 1,389 airports and 886 of these have unpaved runways.

Transport & communications data

- Total roads: 1,408,000 km/874,368 miles
- Total paved roads: 497,306 km/308,827 miles
- Total unpaved roads: 910,694 km/565,541 miles
- Total railways: 49,422 km/30,691 miles
- Major airports: 503
- Cars per 1,000 people: 458
- Mobile phones per 1,000 people: 377
- Personal computers per 1,000 people: 487
- Internet users per 1,000 people: 513

Sources: World Bank and CIA World Factbook

▼ A seaplane at Iconnu Lodge, Yukon Territory.

ROADS

There are 1,408,000 km (874,915 miles) of road in Canada, with about two-thirds of these only suitable for off-road vehicles. The Trans-Canada Highway, running from the Atlantic to the Pacific coast, is 24,459 km (15,198 miles) long. This east-west artery is very important to Canada's economy, with large 'road-train' trucks carrying goods for trade and domestic consumption. Cross-border trade with the USA depends on efficient roads, particularly in the Great Lakes industrial region, where the International Bridge linking Sault St Marie, Ontario, with Sault St Marie, Michigan, eases the flow of commercial traffic.

 Did you know?

Dempster Highway, running from Dawson Highway in the Yukon Territory to Inuvik in the Northwest Territories, and opened in 1978, is one of only two public roads in North America to cross the Arctic Circle.

One of the only roads heading north is the famous Alaskan Highway (more commonly known as the Alcan Highway, standing for Alaska-Canada) in the Yukon Territory, stretching 2,288 km (1,422 miles), from Dawson Creek in British Columbia to Fairbanks in Alaska. This is one of the world's ultimate drives and very popular with tourists, particularly recreational vehicle (RV) owners. It features steep gradients, winding stretches, gravel surfaces and frost heave, which causes the asphalt to 'buckle like a roller coaster'. The highway opened in 1948 and used to be called 'the junkyard of the American automobile', because of the large number of cars left broken down or abandoned along it. There is even a guidebook, called the 'Milepost', and a website to advise motorists on its dangers.

▼ A driver travels on the beautiful but hazardous Alaskan Highway, south of Whitehorse, in Yukon Territory, Canada.

Focus on: Transporting oil and gas

Constructing transport networks across Canada's vast landscape is a major challenge. For instance, Canada has 23,564 km (14,642 miles) of oil pipeline and 74,980 km (46,593 miles) of gas pipeline. Workers have to use a special type of steel when building these pipelines across the earthquake-prone Rocky Mountains. In order to withstand Earth tremors, the pipes need to be flexible, and they also need to be heated when crossing frozen areas. In addition, workers have to avoid laying pipeline foundations in the unstable permafrost (the frozen layer, beneath the soil surface, which is melting in some places). Canada's wildlife also has to be taken into account. For example, some pipelines have been raised to allow migratory reindeer (or caribou) to pass under them. And in Banff National Park, a section of the Trans-Canada Highway has been built with fences to stop wildlife from straying onto the road. Every 1 kilometre (0.6 miles), there is an underpass for animals to use when crossing the highway. There are even overpasses for underpass-wary animals such as cougars, wolves and bears! All these adaptations add greatly to building costs.

RAILWAYS AND SHIPS

The Canadian Pacific Railway is an important transport link between the eastern and western provinces of Canada. Since this first railway opened in 1889, Canada's rail network has expanded considerably and now totals some 49,422 km (30,691 miles) in length. Today it is mainly tourists who take the long east-west trip right across Canada. The journey is a leisurely one, with comfortable sleeping cars and observation domes so that visitors can fully appreciate the magnificent Canadian scenery.

▼ Rail transport is widely used in Canada's cities. This urban rail track is in Vancouver.

Most domestic passenger train journeys in Canada are taken on the regional intercity commuter networks, particularly around the major cities of the Great Lakes-St Lawrence region. With Internet access being introduced on many rail networks, the number of business passengers has increased. In addition to carrying people, the railway network forms a vital link between the wheat fields of the Prairies and the coastal ports, and grain accounts for 25 per cent of all rail freight traffic.

▲ A ship sails through a lock on the St Lawrence Seaway, near Montreal, Quebec, with a cargo of grain.

The St Lawrence Seaway, one of the world's busiest shipping waterways, connects the Great Lakes industrial region with the Atlantic, serving both Canadian and US lake ports. The Seaway (which consists of a network of rivers, seaways and lakes) has been vital for the development of Canada's export trade, which is very important to the Canadian economy. The Seaway is navigable for 3,200 km (1,990 miles), as far as Thunder Bay on Lake Superior, which is linked to Lake Huron by St Mary River. Large sections of the St Lawrence Seaway freeze over during the winter, but it is rare that access to the Great Lakes system is cut off completely.

THE INTERNET
The development of the Internet and mobile phones has brought isolated communities in Canada into much closer contact with the outside world. By 2002, there were an estimated 16.8 million Internet users and approximately 10 million mobile phone users.

In remote territories such as Nunavut, the Internet has enabled a thriving tourist industry to develop, serving travellers who come here in search of the 'wilderness experience'. The Arctic University has also set up a Nunavut campus. Students in Nunavut are almost entirely dependent on the Internet for access to the outside world.

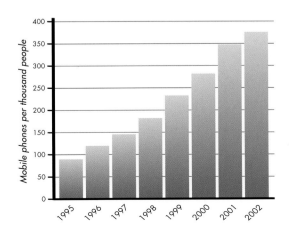

▲ Mobile phone use per 1,000 people, 1995-2002

CHAPTER 10

Education and Health

According to the United Nations Human Development Index, using measures such as education and life expectancy, Canada was ranked fourth in the world in 2004. Adult literacy rates in Canada are among the world's highest, at 99 per cent, and life expectancy averages 79 years.

A WELL-EDUCATED WORKFORCE

School for Canadian children is compulsory and free. In most regions children are taught using the English language, but in Quebec all pupils have the right to be taught in French. The leaving age for most is 16, after which more than three-quarters of students go on to some form of higher education (one of the highest proportions in the world). Canada offers a wide range of both academic and vocational types of higher education to ensure that the country has a well-educated and extremely skilled pool of labour. There are 76 universities and over 200 colleges, most based in the large cities of Toronto, Montreal, Ottawa and Vancouver.

▼ Most schools in the bilingual province of Quebec offer education in both French and English. However, there are also some that teach in only one of the province's two official languages.

The recently opened Nunavut Arctic College has links with other Arctic-based colleges and provides the local Inuit people with access to higher education and life-long learning based on their own culture and traditional values. The Canadian government is also investing in improving access to computers and the Internet for First Nations communities.

▼ Students pass between classes at the University of Toronto. Canada has a well-educated population and many world-class universities.

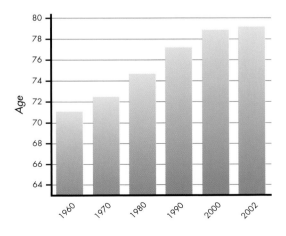

▲ Life expectancy at birth

Education and health data

- Life expectancy at birth male: 76.2
- Life expectancy at birth female: 82.4
- Infant mortality rate per 1,000: 5
- Under five mortality rate per 1,000: 7
- Physicians per 1,000 people: 2.1
- Health expenditure as % of GDP: 9.5%
- Education expenditure as % of GDP: 5.2%
- Primary net enrolment: 99%
- Pupil-teacher ratio, primary: 17
- Adult literacy as % age 15+: 99

Sources: United Nations Agencies and World Bank

HEALTHCARE AND HEALTH PROBLEMS

Canadian healthcare is funded by a national insurance system and the government spends large amounts ensuring that its people enjoy one of the best healthcare systems in the world. Hospitals and health centres in towns and cities are well equipped and there are plenty of doctors available to treat patients. However, there are problems in more remote areas, where it is difficult to get doctors to take up vacant positions. The government is trying to attract more doctors to these areas by offering attractive pay packages with 'isolation pay' or 'hardship benefits'.

Unfortunately, not all Canadians enjoy a high standard of living, and a growing number suffer problems of poverty and deprivation, particularly those on low incomes, including a number of indigenous people. Many First Nations people live on reservations, which often lack the basic services that most other Canadians take for granted. The Canadian government has recognized that there is a particular problem of child poverty and deprivation in reservation communities.

Nationally, Canada has an aging population. Yet the First Nation communities, who make up just 4 per cent of the country's population, include 7 per cent of the country's children below the age of six. Many of these children face problems caused by poverty and ill-health. The government has started to fund new community projects and provide more basic childcare and education programmes in

▼ Inuit children play hockey in the Northwest Territories. Remote communities in Canada often have few healthcare facilities and generally have poorer health than people elsewhere in the country.

reservation areas, but there is still much to be done to improve the life chances for these children.

As in other developed countries, such as the USA and the UK, some of the most common causes of death in modern Canada are cancer, strokes, heart disease and respiratory disease. Despite Canada's excellent health record, a growing number of Canadians eat a lot of high-fat convenience foods and take relatively little exercise, leading to obesity and other health problems. In addition, the country has not escaped the global HIV/AIDS pandemic, with an estimated 50,000 Canadians living with HIV/AIDS and a recorded 500 AIDS-related deaths in 2002. Many of those living with the AIDS virus are able to control their symptoms by taking medication. The government is also funding public education programmes to combat HIV/AIDS, including Internet updates giving guidance on preventative measures.

In a country with higher than average car ownership and vehicle distance travelled, it is not surprising that one of the major causes of death in Canada is road accidents. The rates vary from region to region, with the urban death rate being far lower than that in rural areas. The territory that claims the highest number of road deaths by far is the Yukon. Poor road conditions, long distances, extreme weather and driver fatigue all contribute to the high number of accidents.

 Did you know?

For travellers to Canada, most of the major health hazards are associated with the outdoors. These hazards include 'Beaver Fever' (or Giardia), which is caused by a parasite that is found in soil, food, hot springs, stagnant water and streams. The symptoms include vomiting and stomach cramps.

Focus on: The SARS outbreak

In 2003, Toronto hit the world news, when Canada became the only country outside Asia to report the presence of Severe Acute Respiratory Syndrome (SARS). The outbreak of the deadly virus had earlier been reported in Hong Kong, mainland China and other South-East Asian countries. The disease was thought to have been carried into Canada by a visitor from Asia. The Canadian Health Authority responded quickly by quarantining the infected patients and publishing fact sheets to inform the public and contain the spread. Meanwhile, the World Health Organization advised overseas business travellers and tourists to avoid going to Toronto. This warning lasted only a few weeks.

▲ A family arriving from China walks through Vancouver International Airport, wearing masks, as the fear of SARS spreads to Canada in April 2003.

CHAPTER 11

Culture and Religion

Life in many Canadian towns and cities is similar to life in the USA and the UK. All the same big-name stores and restaurants line the city streets. There are designer clothes shops, cinemas, music festivals, museums, art galleries and sporting venues. Canadians enjoy a wide range of culture and entertainment.

A RICH CULTURAL LIFE

Toronto's theatres are only surpassed by those of London and New York, and well-known Canadian actors include Michael J. Fox and Donald Sutherland. Popular Canadian musical performers, such as Celine Dion, Neil Young, Leonard Cohen, Joni Mitchell, Rush and Sarah McLachlan, have also become famous all over the world. This rich culture has emerged in large cities such as Toronto and Vancouver, where different ethnic groups, including migrants from Asia, follow their own traditions while also feeling a strong sense of identity as Canadian citizens.

▼ Canadian singer Celine Dion is the best-selling female recording artist in the world, with over 125 million album sales. Here, she is seen unveiling a plaque in her honour along Canada's Walk of Fame in Toronto in 1999.

A variety of well-stocked libraries, art galleries and museums are found in all large Canadian cities. However, it is not just the large cities that boast a rich culture. Few small towns in Canada are without a community theatre or arts centre with regular performances and exhibitions. The Canadian government promotes its unique heritage by recognizing the value of shared stories, poetry, knowledge, symbols, languages, customs and traditions. These aspects of Canadian culture are seen as treasures that need to be kept alive and passed on to future generations.

Away from the big cities, in remote rural settlements, there tends to be less ethnic diversity, with more homogenous small communities. Some First Nations people live in government-funded

▲ Some First Nations people, particularly along Canada's western coast, carve totem poles to tell stories about their communities. The figures show the importance of different community members. Each member has a carved symbol that is believed to be associated with a mystical non-human ancestor, often a wolf, a bear, an eagle, a whale, a salmon or a raven.

reservations in rural areas where many follow their original traditions. However, over 50 per cent of First Nations people now live in some of Canada's major cities, including Toronto, and many in the more remote cities such as Winnipeg in the Prairies. These urban aboriginals often face discrimination and social and economic challenges not usually experienced by other city-dwellers. However, with growing awareness and support from the Canadian government, an increasing number of young First Nation Canadians are attracted to the economic benefits and rich cultural diversity of city life.

▲ A fruit and vegetable market in Chinatown, in Toronto. With residents from many different ethnic groups, cities like Toronto and Vancouver are extremely multicultural.

HOLIDAYS AND FESTIVALS

Apart from the annual school and work holidays, Canadians enjoy ten national public holidays as well as many individual provincial celebration days. In total, 250 festivals take place in Canada each year. Some of the national public holidays celebrate particular events, such as Labour Day, which commemorates the early recognition of trade unions in Canada in 1872. Other provincial festivals, such as the Maple Syrup festival in early April, celebrate old customs. The Maple Syrup festival marks the beginning of Spring and the people of Quebec and Ontario follow the tradition, started by the First Nations people, of boiling the sap of the maple tree to make syrup. Chinese New Year festivals are also a familiar feature in January in most Canadian cities.

DIFFERENT RELIGIOUS GROUPS

According to the 2001 census, around 45 per cent of Canadians were Roman Catholic (with the majority of this group living in Quebec), and 28 per cent were Protestants. Within the Protestant population, there are some extreme groups who enjoy the freedom to practise their religion in virtual isolation in this large and sparsely populated country.

For example, the Mennonites, a group originally founded in the early sixteenth

◀ The Canadian Tulip Festival is held in mid-May, in Ottawa. Since the Second World War ended in 1945, the people of Holland have sent 100,000 tulip bulbs to Ottawa each year to show their appreciation of Canada's help during the conflict. Canadian troops helped liberate the Netherlands and the Dutch Royal Family found shelter in Canada during the war. Princess Margriet of the Netherlands, who was born in Ottawa, is shown here at the 50th Canadian Tulip Festival in Ottawa, in 2002.

century in the Netherlands by Menno Simmons, fled from persecution in Europe. One group of Mennonites, known as the Untere, were able to settle in Manitoba and live in peace. This group of Mennonites are relatively liberal. Few still wear their traditional clothes or work on communal farms.

The Ammanites, a more traditional Mennonite group, settled in Ontario, mainly in the Kitchener-Waterloo area to the east of Toronto, but – unlike the Untere – they have shunned much of modern Canadian life. They do not use cars, telephones or modern machinery and can often be seen in their horse-drawn carts in local towns when they come in for supplies, wearing their characteristic dark clothing.

Over the last few decades, waves of immigrants from Middle Eastern, Asian and East African countries have brought their diverse religions with them. A total of 63 different religions, faiths and sects are represented in Canada, and in 2001 there were 34 religions with more than 20,000 members each. In the cities, Muslim, Buddhist, Jewish, Hindu and Sikh communities add to Canada's religious and cultural diversity. There are also a growing number of Canadians who declare themselves as atheist, agnostic, humanist or non-religious. There are now 580,000 Canadian Muslims, making up 2 per cent of the population and representing the fastest-growing rate of membership of any religion in Canada. (In 1991, Muslims made up only 0.9 per cent of the Canadian population.) In contrast, membership of Christian churches is declining, with only 73 per cent of Canadians belonging to either the Roman Catholic or Protestant church in 2001, compared with 83 per cent in 1991.

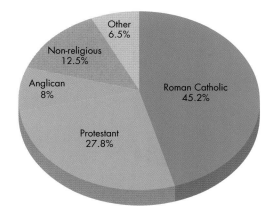

▲ Major religions

Focus on: The Hutterites of Alberta

The Hutterites are an extreme Protestant group who have shunned the modern world almost totally. They refuse to vote, and do not draw pensions or benefits from the Canadian government. Approximately 6,000 Hutterites live in close communities on the Prairie plains of Alberta. They originated in Moravia and their language is Hutterite, a form of German. They live in small communities of approximately 100 people. (When a Hutterite community reaches 150, another community is set up.) All their land is worked communally and they all live in very simple identical houses. Women and children eat together, and the men eat in a separate communal group. The women wear ankle-length, plain, dark-coloured dresses and polka-dot scarves. The men wear dark suits, broad-brimmed hats and beards if they are married.

CHAPTER 12

Leisure and Tourism

In Canada, outdoor activities, such as camping, walking, white-water rafting, canoeing and skiing, are popular. Many Canadian families have cabins in the countryside, where they spend summer holidays. They may also go to these cabins in winter for hunting and skiing trips. Even large cities are within a short drive of open spaces, scenic landscapes and coastal or lakeside beaches. Most towns and villages have a nearby lake or river teeming with fish. And all public parks, beaches and parking areas on main roads have barbecue and picnic facilities.

WINTER SPORTS

Skiing is a popular leisure pursuit in eastern Canada, with its very snowy winters. There are more than 400 ski runs close to Montreal and

Tourism in Canada

- ☐ Tourist arrivals, millions: 20.057
- ☐ Earnings from tourism in US$: 9,700,000,000
- ☐ Tourism as % foreign earnings: 3
- ☐ Tourist departures, millions: 17.705
- ☐ Expenditure on tourism in US$: 9,929,000,000

Source: World Bank

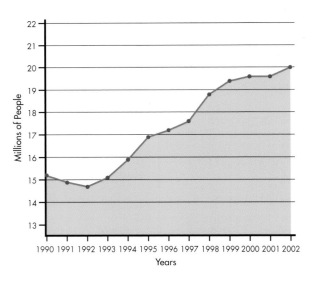

▲ Changes in international tourist arrivals, 1990-2001

◄ Whistler, near Vancouver, in British Columbia, is one of Canada's most popular ski resorts.

the city park, Mount Royal Park, is a particular favourite with families for casual skiing on winter weekends. On a grander scale, skiing resorts in the Rockies, centred around Calgary and Whistler, offer some of the best facilities in the world and attract many European and American visitors.

Many Canadians also enjoy playing ice hockey, and Canada holds a leading position in world ice hockey competitions. The Canadian men's ice hockey team won the gold medal at the Salt Lake City Winter Olympics in 2002.

Calgary was the location for the 1988 Winter Olympics and Vancouver has been chosen as the 2010 destination. Canadians are also well known in world Olympic stadia for swimming, rowing, cycling, trampolining and many other sports. In the 2004 Olympics, held in Athens, they won 12 medals, including three gold.

SIGHT-SEEING AND ACTIVITY HOLIDAYS

Canada is vast, and journeys taken within the country cross a huge variety of landscapes and climates, from the frozen expanses of the Northwest Territories to the much warmer temperatures of Vancouver on the Pacific coast. Canada has a great deal to offer tourists – city destinations like Toronto with its CN Tower and Sky Dome, dramatic sights like Niagara Falls, skiing in the Canadian Rockies, whale-watching on the banks of the St Lawrence, and trekking through wilderness areas.

Canada also has many theme parks, full of 'thrills and spills'. With so much land to spare,

▼ Canada's Adam Van Koeverden wins his men's K1 canoeing 500 metres gold medal at the Athens 2004 Olympic Games.

some of these parks can boast that many of their attractions are the biggest of their kind. The Galaxy Park, near Edmonton, Alberta, is completely climate-controlled, with a huge 2 hectare (5 acre) water park kept at a balmy 30°C (85°F) all year round. In the same complex is 'Ice Palace', which has a national hockey league sized ice rink. The Tomb Raiders' Flying Roller Coaster and other nerve-jarring film-themed rides are all on offer in Toronto's huge Paramount Wonderland theme park.
Tourists from South-East Asia, where thriving economies have increased personal spending

▲ Toronto has many attractions for visitors, including the CN Tower, seen here with Lake Ontario in the foreground. Visitors are whisked to the top of the tower at a frightening 365 m (1,197 feet) per minute – equivalent to the rate of ascent of a jet at take-off!

power, see Canada as a very appealing destination. The Japanese, in particular, are attracted to the leisure resorts and cities of British Columbia, where city holidays in Vancouver and Calgary can be easily combined with visits to the local ski resorts of Calgary, Banff and Lake Louise.

Tourist income is very important to Canada. However, in line with world trends, the number of overseas visitors dropped to a lower level in 2002-2003. Global terrorism, the September 11 attacks on the USA and the SARS outbreak all took their toll on international tourism generally and particularly on travel to North American destinations. Thankfully, these events have not had a long-term effect on tourism and certainly not on travellers from the USA and within Canada.

NATIONAL PARKS

National parks are a major destination for Canadians during their leisure breaks. With such a huge expanse of uninhabited land, the Canadian government has set aside 38 national parks and national park reserves. (The 'reserves' are areas where there are unresolved land claims from indigenous peoples, and they usually become officially designated national parks as soon as the claim is settled.)

The most popular parks are located in the Rocky Mountain provinces, where visitors can enjoy outdoor leisure acitivities including skiing, hiking and camping. The spectacular scenery attracts both Canadians and visitors from all over the world. There are many other national parks all over Canada, and the National Parks and Wilderness Society protects many 'wilderness areas' that are not designated as national parks. The parks are strictly controlled to ensure a balance between visitor access, natural habitats and landscapes so that all are preserved and maintained to co-exist in harmony. Any extractive industries, such as mining or quarrying, are banned in the parks, and visitor access and activities are carefully

monitored. Canada's first national park, a 26 sq km (10 sq mile) area on the north slope of Mount Sulphur in the Rockies, was established in 1885. This area was later expanded and became the famous Banff National Park in 1887.

Focus on: Banff National Park

Banff, the best-known national park in Canada, is part of a UNESCO World Heritage site and covers 20,000 sq km (7,722 sq miles) of the Canadian Rocky Mountains. Its enormous popularity, its ecological and cultural importance, its contribution to the economy and its service to visitors make it unique among Canada's national parks. The park management team has divided the land use into five different zones, with recreational activities tightly restricted in Zones 1, 2 and 3. Zone 4 (only taking up 1 per cent of the land) is the main location for recreational

activities, and Zone 5 (a further 1 per cent of the land) contains the town of Banff and the Lake Louise complex, where most of the park's shops and visitor services are found. Throughout the park, there are instruction and advice notice boards to help ensure the preservation of wildlife habitats and the safety and enjoyment of visitors.

▼ Walkers stop to enjoy the view at the bright blue Moraine Lakes near Lake Louise, in Banff National Park, Alberta, against the backdrop of the Rocky Mountains.

CHAPTER 13

Environment and Conservation

Canada's often inhospitable landscape and climate has helped preserve many of its remote wilderness areas. However, some of these wildernesses contain valuable resources, such as timber, which are in great demand. So Canada is faced with the same dilemma as any resource-rich country – how to balance the need to protect its environment with the demand for jobs and economic development. With continuing pressure for economic development, environmental protection of such a huge country is a growing problem.

THE 'BRAZIL OF THE NORTH'

Approximately 37 per cent of Canada's land area is covered in forest, and deforestation is currently seen as the country's most serious environmental threat. It is estimated that two-thirds of the original 'old growth' forest in British Columbia has been felled. Environmentalists criticize the 'clear cutting' method used, whereby whole hillsides are stripped bare of trees and left open to soil erosion. There is no significant political 'green party' in Canada, but the Forest Processing Association is working with logging companies to encourage more sustainable practices. Non-governmental organizations, such as the Rainforest Conservation Society, also research and publish articles on issues of environmental concern affecting the rainforests of Vancouver Island and criticize the British Columbian government for not doing more to stop the destruction.

POLLUTION PROBLEMS

Only 11 per cent of Canada's land is either populated or cultivated but advances in technology and construction of access routes

▼ A forest on Vancouver Island, British Columbia, where the 'clear cutting' method is being used.

have led to increasing expansion into remote areas. Canada has relatively few manufacturing industries for its size. However, many Canadians own cars and most of them make a large number of car journeys. So the rate of atmospheric pollution by greenhouse gases per person is significantly high. On the positive side, Canada has

pledged, in line with most developed countries, to reduce its CO_2 emissions. In addition, Montreal was the location of a 1987 international summit at which several countries agreed to phase out the use of chloro-fluoro-carbons (CFCs) in aerosols, refrigerators and other products. (CFCs destroy the protective ozone layer in the Earth's atmosphere for up to 100 years after they are released, and Canada had already banned use of CFCs in aerosols by 1978.)

However, even if the environmental damage caused by Canada's own economic development is reduced to a minimum, global pollution in the atmosphere and oceans would still affect its delicately balanced ecosystems, particularly in the tundra and Arctic regions of Nunavut and the Northwest Territories. These frozen lands, and the habitats they support, are becoming increasingly vulnerable to climate change, and ice sheets are thinning as temperatures rise.

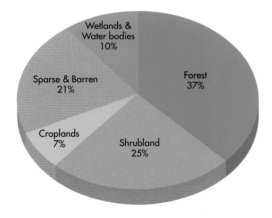

▲ Habitat type as percentage of total area

Environmental and conservation data

📁 Forested area as % total land area: 37

📁 Protected area as % total land area: 6.3

📁 Number of protected areas: 5,285

SPECIES DIVERSITY

Category	Known species (1992-02)	Threatened species (2002)
Mammals	193	14
Breeding birds	440	8
Reptiles	39	2
Amphibians	42	1
Fish	128	16
Plants	3,270	1

Source: World Resources Institute

 A herd of caribou runs across an open field in the Northwest Territories. Caribou are a very important source of meat and skins for the Inuit. Their breathable, waterproof hide is essential to hunters living in snowbound communities.

THREATS TO WILDLIFE

In the nineteenth century, the buffalo was almost hunted to extinction in Canada and the northern USA by Plains Indians and by white hunters. Historians have been very critical of this destruction but the same story is being repeated today with the caribou (or reindeer) that roam the frozen wilderness of northern Canada. Their numbers have fallen from approximately 2.5 million in the 1940s to some 700,000 today. And the caribou is just one of the animals in danger of extinction in modern Canada.

In 2004, newspapers around the world showed pictures of baby seals being clubbed to death off the coasts of Newfoundland and Labrador. This was reported to be the biggest cull of seals for 50 years. The media reports caused anger among wildlife conservation groups. But if seal numbers are not controlled, the seals will in turn decimate the fish stocks in Canada's east coast waters. For these reasons, the Canadian government allows hunters to kill 350,000 young seals each year. In this case, critics felt that the culling was excessive

and was linked with the high prices paid by the fashion industry for seal pelts, which are made into a range of items, including coats, jackets, boots and bags. However, the government argues that the seal culling industry (worth 20 million Canadian dollars a year) is needed to support Canada's economically troubled eastern seaboard coastal towns, particularly those of Newfoundland. These east coast towns have suffered economic losses from the decline in the fishing industry, mainly brought about by the cod fishing ban in 1992. Over 40,000 people lost their jobs and property values dropped in the early 1990s, as people tried to get out of the area to find new jobs. Recovery on the eastern seaboard continues to be very slow.

Did you know?

According to the WWF (formerly known as the World Wildlife Fund) summer sea ice in the Arctic is currently decreasing by 9.2 per cent each decade, and the polar bear and some seal species could be extinct by 2026.

Focus on: Polar bears

Canada has about 15,000 polar bears, the largest group in any one country. The bears were once hunted almost to the point of extinction, but a treaty signed by the Arctic countries (Canada, the USA, Norway, Greenland and Russia) in 1967 helped protect them. Unfortunately, polar bears are again under threat – this time because of global warming and industrial pollution. Many Canadian polar bears hunt in the Hudson-St James Bay region, where – because of global warming – the frozen waters are now melting three weeks earlier than they did in 1980, cutting down the polar bears' hunting time significantly. In addition, there are many industrial pollutants in the water. These pollutants are eaten by the fish, and, when the polar bears eat the fish, the pollutants are concentrated in the bears' bodies. These poisons damage the bears' immune systems. Scientists have recorded a significant decrease in the size and weight of polar bears in recent years and fewer cubs are being born. The Inuit people are allowed to hunt polar bears, according to a quota system.

◄ Two zoologists take samples from tranquillized polar bears to check their pesticide levels, at Hudson Bay, Manitoba.

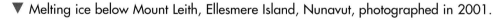

▼ Melting ice below Mount Leith, Ellesmere Island, Nunavut, photographed in 2001.

CHAPTER 14

Future Challenges

At the beginning of the twenty-first century, Canada is a very prosperous, stable country. It has a low crime rate and is ranked in the lowest 20 countries of the world for reported murders. However, it also faces a number of economic, political, social and environmental challenges.

A STRONG ECONOMY?

Canada's export trade is very strong, and China has become one of Canada's main customers. (Exports to China are said to have risen 75 per cent in the past few years.) However, over-dependence on the export of raw materials could cause economic problems in the long term, particularly if the price of raw materials were to collapse. Expanding its manufacturing base would be a good way for Canada to diversify its economy, but labour and production costs in Canada are relatively high. As a result, some manufacturers have been moving their production to Mexico, where costs are lower.

SOCIAL AND ENVIRONMENTAL PROBLEMS

In an effort to balance national budgets, taxes and prices in Canada have been rising and many people on low incomes have been

▼ Non-violent protesters march to the Peace Bridge, which links Fort Erie, Ontario, Canada, and Buffalo, New York, USA, in 2001 to protest against the Free Trade Area of Americas (FTAA) and North Atlantic Free Trade Agreement (NAFTA). Many US companies are leaving Canada, taking jobs with them, because the free trade agreements mean there are fewer tax advantages for them in Canada.

experiencing increasing financial problems. Welfare payments have also been cut, causing many indigenous people living in marginal, extreme environments, such as the Northwest Territories, to abandon their traditional lifestyles (which were supported by welfare payments) and move to Canada's main cities in search of reliable work. With all Canada's main cities being located in a belt close to the US border, this urban concentration may, in the future, start to put too much pressure on land and resources in and around this US border region.

There are also some problems between particular groups, such as the First Nations people and the 'newer' Canadians (mostly of European origin), often over access to resources. The present government is working hard to bridge these divisions.

Canada is well known for encouraging a multicultural society. But, with a growing number of economic immigrants, and a government that has been accused of being too lax in controlling the inward flow of people, public unease at Canada's immigration policy

has been rising. Canada has a strict immigration policy for anyone applying to come in through official channels, but critics say that, with such a long border and coastline, Canada has too many gaps through which people can enter illegally. The Canadian government is trying to address this problem by working in partnership with the US government.

POLITICAL DIVISION

The political separation of Quebec from the rest of Canada is an issue that is not likely to disappear. The people of Quebec have had two referendums on this question, and those in favour of independence have been narrowly defeated. However, if the fight continues and they win, the Canadian government will lose its largest province, which also produces a great deal of Canada's energy (in the form of hydro-electric power) and much of its industrial output. Keeping Quebec within Canada is going to be a major challenge for the future.

▼ A Canadian immigration officer gathers illegal Asian migrants as they prepare to board buses, in Gold River, British Columbia, in 1999.

Timeline

c. 25,000 BC Indigenous peoples start settling the land now known as Canada, mainly via the 'land bridge' that existed between present-day Russia and Alaska.

1497 John Cabot, an Italian explorer, is given permission by Henry VII of England to set sail to Canada.

1534 Jacques Cartier, a French explorer, pioneers the first European settlement in Canada.

1670 King Charles II of England grants a Royal Charter to the Hudson's Bay Company for trapping and mineral rights on the land draining into Hudson Bay (known as Rupert's Land).

1759 The French are defeated by the British on the Plains of Abraham, just outside Quebec City. The French are then forced to give up the land they hold around the St Lawrence area and the Quebec settlements.

1763 France gives up all the lands it holds in North America, including Quebec.

1846 The Oregon Treaty sets the 49th parallel as the boundary between Canada and the rest of North America to the south, the United States.

1867 The North American Act creates the first confederation of Canada, which includes Nova Scotia, New Brunswick and the area then known as Canada.

1905 Alberta and Saskatchewan join the confederation.

1917 As allies of the British in the Second World War, Canadian soldiers are victorious at Vimy Ridge.

1949 Canada becomes a founder member of NATO.

1976 The Parti Quebecois wins the provincial election in Quebec and French is made the official language in the province of Quebec.

Canada joins the G8 group of industrialized nations.

Montreal hosts the Olympic Games.

1982 Canada reaches the final stage of independence when the UK government transfers to Canada all powers relating to Canada in British law.

1988 Calgary hosts the Winter Olympics.

1992 Canada withdraws all its troops from European bases.

1994 NAFTA agreement between Canada, USA and Mexico comes into force.

1995 The people of Quebec narrowly reject separation and independence from the rest of Canada.

1999 Nunavut is created as a separate territory.

2003 Paul Martin becomes Canadian prime minister.

Hurricane Juan hits Nova Scotia and Prince Edward Island, the worst hurricane to hit an inland location so far north.

SARS outbreak in Toronto.

2004 At the Olympic Games in Greece, Canada wins 12 medals including three gold.

Glossary

Aboriginal title Land that was previously accepted as belonging to aboriginal or indigenous groups.

Albedo effect An effect created when the sun's rays are reflected off a white surface, reducing the amount of solar radiation.

Allies Britain and her Allies in the First and Second World Wars.

Anglophile Someone who favours English culture.

Aquaculture Fish farming.

Asylum seeker A refugee who claims the right to live in safety in another country because of persecution in his or her own land.

Autonomous Independent or self-governing.

Bilateral aid Aid that is given directly, usually by a more developed to a less developed country in the form of a single project where there are benefits for both countries.

Bituminous Containing bitumen, a tar-like substance that is a mixture of hydrocarbons.

Clear cutting Felling all the trees and removing all the vegetation from a forested area.

Colony A country or land that has been taken over by an economic power, usually in order to exploit its resources.

Confederation A union of states under a single central government.

Cultural identity Customs and features of one particular group of peoples.

Democracy A system of government in which the people vote for representatives in elections.

Earth Summit A meeting of industrialized nations, held in Kyoto, Japan, in 1997, to discuss environmental issues.

Eskimo The name (meaning 'meat eater') given to the Inuit people of Northern Canada by the Algonquin people.

Federalism A system of government in which several states are united under one government but remain independent in their internal affairs.

First Nations people Groups of original settlers who adapted their lifestyles to the four distinct local environments of the Pacific coast, the Plains, the St Lawrence Valley and the North-East Woodlands. Within these groups, there are many tribes.

Global warming The gradual warming of the Earth's atmosphere as a result of carbon dioxide emissions and other greenhouse gases trapping heat.

Gross Domestic Income All the income earned from industries based in a country and exports produced in that country.

HIV/AIDS Human Immunodeficiency Virus (HIV) is a deadly virus spread by unprotected sex or contaminated needles or blood supplies. It can develop into Acquired Immuno-Deficiency Syndrome (AIDS), which is fatal.

Homogeneous Consisting of parts of the same kind.

Hurricane A violent storm exceeding a wind force of 75 mph (65 knots), usually in tropical areas.

Indigenous Born in a region, belonging naturally to a place.

Inuit Canadian indigenous tribes of the Arctic regions.

NAFTA (North Atlantic Free Trade Association) A trading group linking the USA, Canada and Mexico.

NATO (The North Atlantic Treaty Organization) A defensive military alliance, established in 1949, that includes the USA, Canada and many European countries.

Permafrost The permanently frozen subsurface layer in Arctic lands.

Prairies The large region of rich agricultural land, famed for cereal production, spanning Alberta, Saskatchewan, Manitoba and some US states.

Provinces Principal administrative divisions of a country.

Quebecois French-speaking residents of Quebec Province.

Refugee A person taking refuge in a safe place from persecution, war or a natural disaster.

Reservation An area of land reserved for occupation by aboriginal people such as North American Indians.

RV (Recreational Vehicle) A vehicle such as the large motor homes used by travellers.

SARS (Severe Acute Respiratory Syndrome) A virus that caused a high death toll in Hong Kong and the Far East during 2003.

SUV (Sports Utility Vehicle) A four-wheel-drive jeep-type vehicle that can be used both off and on the road.

Tectonic plate A large section of the Earth's crust. The Earth is thought to have 12 major plates. Earthquakes and volcanic activity are common along their boundaries.

Totem pole A pole used by some North American Indian groups to tell a tribal story through its carved images.

Trade surplus The amount by which the value of a country's exports exceeds the costs of its imports.

UN (United Nations) A large group of countries that joined together in 1945, at the end of the Second World War, to promote peace and co-operation all over the world.

Wilderness A big area of land that is almost completely unaffected by human activity.

Further Information

BOOKS TO READ

Canada
Sally Garrington
(Evans Brothers, 2005)

World Tour of Canada
Sean Dolan
(Raintree, 2003)

The Changing Face of Canada
Catherine and D'Arcy Little
(Hodder Wayland, 2004)

Nations of the World – Canada
Greg Nickles and Nicki Walker
(Raintree, 2003)

USEFUL WEBSITES

www.theglobeandmail.com/
Daily newspaper reports, mainly from Toronto.

www.nunavuttourism.com/
Information about developing Nunavut tourism.

www.eia.doe.gov/emeu/cabs/canada.html –
Up-to-date facts about Canada.

www.niagarafrontier.com
Details about Niagara Falls.

www.ocanada.ca/climate/regional.php
Details about the climate of Canada.

www.cdli.ca/CITE/totem-poles.htm
Information about totem poles and their origins.

www.nationmaster.com/country/ca/
Basic facts and figures about Canada.

Index

Page numbers in **bold** indicate pictures.

acid rain 35, **35**
Afghanistan 13, **13**, 35, 36, **37**
Africa 37
aid, overseas 36, 37, **37**
air travel 38, **38**
Alaska 4, 15, 29, 35, 39
Alberta 11, 12, 26, **26**, 27, 49, 52, **53**
Algonqin people 8, 20
Ammanites 49
Annan, Kofi **34**
Arctic Ocean 4, 56
army 13, **13**, 35, 36, **36**
Atlantic Ocean 4, 9, 14, 17, 21, 32, 39, 41

Banff National Park 40, 53, **53**
Britain 6, 9, 10, 13, 22, 24, 30, 35
British Columbia **10**, 11, **14**, 15, 16, 19, 20, **20**, 22, 28, 29, 32, 39, **50**, 52, 54, **54, 59**
buffalo 8, 56
Bush, President George W. **22**, 35

Cabot, John **8**, 9
Calgary 13, 51, 52
caribou 6, 40, 56, **56**
cars 28, 39, **39**, 45, 55
China 19, 21, 26, 30, 45, 58
Chinatown districts 19, **19**, 47
climate 6, 13, 15 16, 17, 21, 28, 38, 55
coal 26, 27
colonization 9, 10, 11
communications 38, 41, 43
confederation, Canadian 11, 22, 24
copper 28, **28**
crops 8, 13, 16, **16**, 28, 31, **31**,
culture 20, 22, 35, 43, 46, **46**, 47, **47**
currency 6, 30

deforestation 29, **29**, 54, **54**
Dion, Celine 46, **46**

diseases 45, **45**

economy 13, 19, 21, 25, 30, 31, 32, 33, 39, 41, 56, 58
education 6, 25, 42, **42**, 43, **43**,
electricity 27, 28
employment 6, 20, 25, 30, 31
energy 26, **26**, 27, **27**, 28
environmental problems 17, 26, 27, 29, 31, 32, 34, 35, **35**, 54, **54**, 55, 56, 57, **57**, 58, 59
Europe 12, 13, 18, 31, 35, 49
explorers 8, 9, 10
exports 28, 30, 34, 41, 58

farming 8, 13, 14, 16, **16**, 31, **31**, 37
festivals 21, 46, 48, **48**
film industry 33
First Nations people 6, 8, 9, 10, 11, 12, 18, 20, **20**, 27, 31, 43, 44, 47, **47**, 59
First World War 13
fish farms 32, **32**
fishing **4**, 8, 9, 28, **35**, 50, 56
forests 16, 29, **29**, 30, 35 54, **54**
fossil fuels 26, 27, 31
France 6, 9, 10, 13, 21, 22, 24, 35
French-speaking Canadians 6, 18, 21, 24, 25, **25**, 42
fur trapping 6, 9, **9**, 12, 20, 28

gas 26, 27, 40
glaciers 14, 15
global warming 17, 55, 57, **57**
gold 13, 28
government 22, 23, 24, 25, 35, 43, 44, 45, 47, 56
Great Lakes 9, 14, 16, 17, 18, 28, 31, 33, 39, 41

Haida people 20, **20**
healthcare 6, 44, 45, 45
HIV/AIDS 37
Holland 9, **48**

Hudson Bay 9, 14, **57**
Hudson's Bay Company 10, **10**, 11, **11**, 12
hunting 6, 8, 17, 50, 56, 57
Hutterites 49
hydro-electric power 26, 27, **27**, 33

immigrants 6, 13, 18, 19, **19**, 59, **59**
imports 30, 34
income 25, 30, 32
independence, Canadian 6, 13, 35
India 37
indigenous people 8, 9, 10, 11, 23
Internet, the 41, 43, 45
Inuit people 6, 8, 17, 18, 20, 23, 43, **44**, 57
Iraq 26, 35, 36
Iroquois people 8, 9

Japan 26, 27, 30, 31, 33

Kyoto Summit 26, 27

Labrador 56
lakes 14, 15, 21, **21**, 28, 38, 41
land disputes 12, 20, 23, 52
languages 18, 24, 25, **25**, 35 42
leisure pursuits 50, **50**, 51, 52, **52**, 53, **53**
life expectancy 42, 43
living standards 6, 21, 42, 44

MacDonald, John Alexander 23
Manitoba 11, 12, 49, **57**
manufacturing industries 31, 32, **32**, 33, **33**, 37, 55, 58
Martin, Prime Minister Paul 22, **22**, **34**
Mennonites 49
metals 13, 28, 33, **33**
Mexico 15, **22**, 30, 33, 58
minerals 28
mobile phones 41
Montreal 5, 17, 20, 21, 25, 33, 42, 50, 51, 55

mountains 14, **14**, 15, 16, 50, **50**, 51, 53, **53**
Muslims 49

NAFTA 30, **58**
national parks 40, 52, 53, **53**
NATO 13, 35
New Brunswick 11
Newfoundland 4, 9, 11, 17, 56
Niagara Falls 15, **15**, 51
North America 8, 9, 24, 26, 33
North Pole 16
Northwest Territories 5, 10, 15, 17, **17**, 23, 39, **44**, 51, 55, 56, 59
Nova Scotia 11, **35**
nuclear power 26, 27
Nunavut **4**, 5, 12, 15, 20, 23, 41, 55, **57**

oceans 4, 9, 14, 16, 17, 21, 28
oil 26, 27, 35
oil sands 26, **26**
Ontario **5**, 11, 12, 21, 27, 28, 33, 48
Oregon Treaty 22
Ottawa 5, 21, 36, 42, **48**

Pacific Ocean 4, 16, 21, 32, 39
paper industry 30, 31, 32, **32**
permafrost 15, 17, 40
physical geography 6
polar bears 17, **17**, 56, 57, **57**
pollution 35, **35**, 55, 57
population 5, 6, 18, 19, 20, 21, 30
ports 11, 21, 35, 41
Prairie Provinces 10, 11, 12, 13, 14, 16, 16, **41**, 47
Prince Edward Island 11
Protestants 48, 49

Quebec 6, 11, 18, 21, 22, 24, 25, **25**, 27, 33, 42, **42**, 48, 59
Queen Charlotte Islands 20, **20**

railways 12, **12**, 21, 31, 38, 40, **40**, 41
rainfall 16, 29
religions 35, 48, 49
resources 26, 28, **28**, 29, **29**, 30
rivers 14, 15, 27, **27**, **35**
roads 21, 39, **39**
Rocky Mountains 12, **14**, 15, 16, 40, 52, 53, **53**
Roman Catholics 48, 49
Rupert's Land 11, 12
Russia 4, 13, 26, 57
Rwanda **36**

SARS 45, **45**, 52
Saskatchewan 11, 12, **17**, 31, **31**
seals 17, 56
Second World War 13, **48**
service industries 32
settlers 6, 9, 10, 11, 12, 13, 18
Seven Years' War 9
skiing 50, **50**, 51, 52
social problems 6, 44, 45, 58
solar power 27
South-East Asia 4, 21, 30, 45, 52
sport 50, **50**, 51, **51**
St Lawrence region 16, 17, 18, 41
St Lawrence River 8, 10, 11, 51
St Lawrence Seaway 14, 21, 31, 33, 41, **41**
steel industry 33, **33**
Sudan 37

Tanzania 37
terrorism 34, 35, 52
theme parks 51, 52
timber industry 28, 29, **29**, 30, 54, **54**
Toronto 5, **5**, 17, 20, 21, **21**, 25, 33, 42, **43**, 45, **46**, 47, 51, 52, **52**
totem poles 8, **47**
tourism **15**, 33, 40, 45, 50, **50**, 51, 52, **52**, 53, **53**
trade 9, 10, **11**, 12, 30, 31, 33, 34, 35, 39, 58
transport 12, **12**, 31, 33, 38, **38**, 39, **39**, 40, **40**, 41, **41**
Trudeau, Pierre 23, 24

UN 13, 21, **34**, 35, 36, 42
universities 25, 41, 42, 43, **43**
USA 4, 5, 6, 13, 14, 15, 19, 21, 22, 26, 27, 28, 30, 31, 33, 35, 39, 45, 46, 52, 57, 59
Utrecht Treaty 9

Vancouver 5, 13, 16, 19, **19**, 21, 31, 33, 37, 40, 42, **45**, 46, 47, **50**, 51
Vancouver Island **10**, 29, **32**, 54, **54**
Vikings 8
Vimy Ridge, Battle of 13

wheat 13, **16**, 31, **31**, 37, 41
wilderness areas 5, 6, 14, 17, **17**, 26, 28, 41, 51, 52
wildlife 6, 17, **17**, 35, 40, 56, **56**, 57, **57**
wind power 27
Winnipeg **11**, 47

Yukon Territory 10, 11, 13, 21, 28, **38**, 39, **39**, 45

About the Author

Heather Blades has taught at Deepings School, South Lincolnshire, for the past 15 years. She has also been an examiner and moderator for over 10 years. She has written a number of series for young people, including 'People, Places and Themes' and 'Geography Matters' (both published by Heinemann). She has travelled in Canada, especially in Ontario and Quebec.